An Alien Stole My Skateboard

A Comedy

Randall Lewton

A SAMUEL FRENCH ACTING EDITION

SAMUEL FRENCH

FOUNDED 1830

SAMUELFRENCH-LONDON.CO.UK
SAMUELFRENCH.COM

FOR AMATEUR PRODUCTION ENQUIRIES

UNITED KINGDOM AND WORLD
EXCLUDING NORTH AMERICA
plays@SamuelFrench-London.co.uk
020 7255 4302/01

Each title is subject to availability from Samuel French,

depending upon country of performance.

AN ALIEN STOLE MY SKATEBOARD

First performed at Calday Grange Grammar School,
West Kirby, with the following cast:

Bryn Masters/Prince Erfa	Bryn Roberts
Snithan	Mark Knoop
Don Glastonbury	Mark Griffith
Shaun	Nicholas Teige
Dwimor	Richard McLean
Thor	David Evans
Daisy Glastonbury	Liz Farrall
Hash Glastonbury	Daniel Meigh
King Fruma	Tim Roberts
Jon	Jonathan Bloor
Jan	Stuart Welton
Crone	Penelope Denson
Grongo	Philip Evans
Trum	Andrew Moore
Mr Westmorland	Silas Edmonds
Man from "The Moonlight Zone"	Spencer Wakelam
Cook	Ben Gladden
Mithgrun	Matthew Jones
Headmaster	Bill McLachlan
Warriors/Guards	Chris Dennett
	David Edmonds
	Ian Hall
	Paul Toomey
	David Cookson
	Robin Chubb
	Adam Darker
	Keith Henry

SYNOPSIS OF SCENES

CHARACTERS

Earth
Bryn Masters, our hero
Don Glastonbury, his friend
Shaun, another friend
Daisy Glastonbury, Don's mother
Hash Glastonbury, Don's father
Jon
Jan
Mr Westmorland
Headmaster
Man from "The Moonlight Zone"
Schoolboys

Wuldor
Prince Erfa
King Fruma, his father
Dwimor, a wizard
Snithan, brother to the king
Thor, an apprentice
A Crone, Thor's mother
Trum, Chief Thrill
Grongo, Erfa's companion
Two Suppliants
Cook
Mithgrun, a boring old Thrill
Royal Guards, Snithan's Warriors, Thrills

AUTHOR'S NOTES

The Cast
As printed, there are many more male than female roles in the play, reflecting our original production. There is no reason, however, why many of the characters should not become female in your production. The following could be changed with only minor alterations to the script being necessary:

Dwimor	Thor	Grongo
Jon	Jan	Headmaster
Some Warriors	Some Guards	Peasants
Trum	Mithgrun	Thrills
Cook	Roy	

Sets
There are many different scenes in the play and to ensure that scene changes are quick it is best not to have elaborate sets. Items of furniture which can be brought on and off the stage quickly can suggest a setting. We also used free-standing cut-outs made of hardboard as backgrounds.

Don's bedroom: bedspread and pillow on rostrum, "wall" with
      dungeons and dragons posters, table with games equipment
Royal palace: wall hangings with royal crest attached to curtains
Snithan's castle: cut-out castle windows on rostra
Outside school: cut-out school building in distance
Plains of Guma: rocks, cut-out mountains in distance
Snithan's kitchen: table, cut-out kitchen shelves and oven

If you have a cyclorama, different coloured "skies" for the scenes on Earth and on Wuldor are effective.

Staging
We used a stage with proscenium and an extension built out into the audience. The play would work equally well in the round.

The Scruffs
Warning: they will become a producer's nightmare. Ours were of several different types. Some were simply large woollen bobbles made in the

normal way. Others were made from rubber balls covered in glue and then rolled in four inch pieces of wool. The former were suitable for attaching to clothing, wires and sticks to be used as puppets, while the latter bounced well and were used mainly at the end of Scene 5. Both types were given stick-on eyes and other features. The nightmare part comes when they are first introduced into your rehearsals. They are irresistible and will start appearing in every scene. Your cast will give them names and want to take them home. You will learn to hate them. The audience will love them though, so they are worth it in the end.

Costumes

Most of the requirements are fairly obvious. Wuldor is a Tolkien-inspired planet and its inhabitants should be dressed as in the many fighting fantasy books and comics which are readily available. On Earth, you might have trouble finding authentic loon pants.

ACT I

Scene 1

A barren landscape

The lighting is dim. Sinister pulsating music

Prince Erfa appears striding cautiously, looking to L *and* R. *He looks like a fighting fantasy hero, wearing red boots and loin-cloth/trunks, a belt made of gold discs and a collar of the same design. He holds a sword at the ready*

Two Warriors enter from the opposite side, barring his path. He stops. Two more appear behind him, then another two surround him completely. They brandish fearsome weapons. The music builds up in pace and excitement. They attack. Using cunning, skill and strength, Erfa defeats them all

He limps off, wounded

The Lights fade to Black-out

Scene 2

Don's bedroom

In the darkness we hear Shaun's voice

Shaun Are you there? Why is it so dark? Hallo? Don? Ouch! (*He trips*)

Don appears

What's going on?
Don Sorry, Shaun. It's the generator. It's packed in again. Dad's trying to fix it.
Shaun (*getting up*) Why don't you get your power from the electricity board like everyone else?

Don It's my parents. They don't approve of nuclear power stations because of the radioactive waste and they don't approve of ordinary power stations because of the acid rain, so they won't use electricity from the national grid.

The Lights come up to reveal Don's bedroom. There are Fighting Fantasy posters on the walls and game equipment on a table

Shaun So you have your own generator?
Don Yes, it runs on goat dung.
Shaun How many goats have you got?
Don Just the one.
Shaun Does ... it ... I mean ... how much ...?
Don We have a lot of power cuts.
Shaun Is Bryn here yet?
Don No, I told him eight o' clock. He probably won't turn up.
Shaun Well, fantasy role-playing games — are they really suitable entertainment for Bryn? I would have thought he'd have been happier with a bit of weight-training or American football.
Shaun How do you mean?
Don He spends all his time on that skateboard of his. He's not exactly cerebral, is he?
Shaun You mean he's thick?
Don Well, it's just that these games need imagination, sensitivity, strategy, organization, inventiveness. He won't enjoy it, will he?
Shaun He will be a bit disappointed when he finds out the fighting's all done on paper with dice.
Don Why didn't you *explain*?
Shaun He'll be OK. He's a good laugh.

Daisy Glastonbury enters with Bryn, who carries a skateboard. She wears clothes reminiscent of the 1960s and carries a tray with cakes, etc.

Daisy Donovan, didn't you hear the doorbell, darling? Your friend has been standing on the doorstep for ages. What with your father up to his knees in goat droppings and me bottling the nettle wine, he could have been there all night.
Don Sorry Bryn.
Bryn That's OK, Don. It's not raining hard.
Daisy Oh don't call him "Don", please. I'd never have called him

Donovan if I'd thought people would shorten it to Don. Don sounds like a sports commentator.

Bryn Sorry.

Don Don't worry. They named me Donovan after the folk singer.

Bryn What folk singer?

Pause

Don Donovan.

Pause

Bryn Oh yeah.

Shaun I've never heard of him.

Daisy sings a few lines of "Sunshine Superman" by Donovan

Don (*moaning*) Mum! Honestly. You've been watching that *Woodstock* video again, haven't you?

Daisy starts singing "Woodstock" by Joni Mitchell

Daisy Oh, I brought you up some fairy cakes. I'm very into baking at the moment. Baking's very *real*. Would you like something to drink?

Shaun Yes, please, Mrs Glastonbury.

Daisy Oh, Shaun, you're always so formal. How many times have I told you to call me Daisy?

Shaun Sorry.

Daisy I'll get the drinks.

Daisy exits

Shaun Your parents are amazing, Donovan. They're so liberal.

Don Yes, I know. It's a bit embarrassing sometimes. They're still living in the nineteen sixties.

Bryn You mean sex and drugs and rock 'n' roll?

Don Well, they're both over forty, so they've given up sex. But they play Jimi Hendrix records all the time.

Bryn And I expect they take drugs too.

Don No, I don't think so. They've probably given that up as well.

Bryn But what about those plants in your hall?

Don What about them?

Bryn Marijuana, aren't they?
Don Don't be daft. They're geraniums. Shall we get on with the game?

They sit at the table

Shaun But, Don, what about last Christmas when they were both arrested
and you had to stay with us?
Don That was political.
Shaun "Illegal possession" it said in the local paper.
Don Well, the police had to make up something like that, didn't they?
They couldn't admit that they'd flung them in gaol because of their
naïve political idealism, could they? They've only got a criminal record
because someone found out they'd joined Greenpeace.
Shaun OK, Don.
Don I mean, yes, when they were younger, they have told me that they did
experiment with — certain substances ... well, they all did in the sixties
... and now just because they're against fox-hunting and they have
psychedelic wallpaper in the bathroom and they wear silly woolly hats,
people think they smoke pot all the time. Well, they don't. Do you
understand? My parents don't take drugs. There are no drugs in this
house.

Bryn reaches for a cake

But I wouldn't eat the fairy cakes if I were you.

Daisy enters with drinks

Daisy Anybody want some Coke?
Don She means Coca-Cola. Why don't you call it by its proper name?
Daisy You're very excited, Donovan. Stay cool.

*Daisy takes a fairy cake and leaves, singing "Eight Miles High" by The
Byrds*

Don I don't know how to tell them I'm joining the Young Conservatives.
Bryn What about the game, Don?
Don Yes. Let's get started. Is this the first time you've played role-playing
games?
Bryn Yes, I'm more of a footballer, really. Shaun says there's fighting in
it though.

Don Well, yes. We get to that later. The first thing we have to do is sort out your character.

Bryn There's nothing wrong with my character.

Shaun Well, I could think of a few improvements.

Don No. No. Not your *real* character, the character you are going to play in the game.

Bryn It's like acting in a play?

Don Well, a bit, yes. You see we use these books and the dice here to build up a character for you and you play that character. Shaun and I already have our characters and when we've created yours you keep it, tonight, tomorrow and whenever we play the game.

Bryn Tomorrow? I thought we were playing football tomorrow. I don't want to sit indoors all day.

Don Yes, I think your character had better be some kind of a man of action. A warrior maybe. I don't think they have skateboarders.

Bryn (*looking at the booklet*) How about something like this? (*He points at the illustration*)

Don Well, I was thinking ... er ... look here.

Bryn and Don go into a huddle over the booklet

A man in a grey suit walks into the scene

Only Shaun notices him. He is puzzled

Man (*addressing the audience*) Three boys in a suburban bedroom engrossed in a world of fantasy, a world of heroes and dragons, a world where good and evil meet in battle across a landscape of the imagination.

Shaun Don, a man's just walked into your bedroom.

The others ignore him

Man A scene repeated in houses throughout the land but for these boys this will turn out to be no ordinary game.

Shaun He's talking to himself.

He is ignored again

Man They will find themselves catapulted into a world beyond imagination. They are about to take a nightmare journey, a journey to (*dramatic chord*) the Moonlight Zone.

The man walks off

Shaun stares after him

Don Shaun! Shaun! Roll the dice.
Shaun But — but ...
Don What's the matter?
Shaun Didn't you ...? Just then ...?
Don The dice. We want to get started.
Shaun I don't like this. Something strange is going to happen.

Black-out. Shaun screams

Don Shaun, what's the matter with you? It's only the generator again.

Don switches on his torch, making his face look creepy. Shaun screams again

Bryn Shaun!
Shaun What?! What?! (*He is a nervous wreck*)
Don ⎫
         ⎬ (*together*) Roll the dice!
Bryn ⎭

Torches off. Black-out

SCENE 3

The royal palace

A fanfare, followed by ceremonial music

Guards and Attendants lead in a procession. Two thrones are placed. King Fruma enters last of all and sits on the throne. All grovel to the king who is very old and walks with a stick

Fruma I sent for the prince half an hour ago. Why is he not in attendance?

The Guards and Attendants look at each other nervously

  Well?

Guard 1 His royal highness, the Prince Erfa, is not in the palace, your majesty.

The King rises and approaches the Guard

Fruma Not in the palace? Has there been a thorough search?

Guard 1 Yes, your majesty. Parties of your majesty's guards are seeking him through the city.

Fruma He was supposed to be under supervision fifty-three hours a day. I entrusted him to the court magician's care. Where is Dwimor, the old wizard? Summon him.

Guard 1 Summon Dwimor, the old wizard!

This is echoed by voices in the distance. Fruma turns towards his throne

Dwimor is sitting on the throne gazing into a crystal ball

Fruma Dwimor! (*To the audience*) The old wizard.

Dwimor Pardon me, your majesty. I have been observing emanations from another world at the end of the galaxy. Fascinating.

Dwimor hands the crystal ball to Fruma for him to look at. We hear the "Neighbours" theme tune. The King is impatient

Fruma Dwimor! You were entrusted with the care of Prince Erfa. He cannot be found. If anything has happened to him ...

Dwimor He is safe.

Fruma You know where he is?

Dwimor No, I was just trying to reassure you.

Fruma Well, you failed. If anything has happened to my son, you will pay for it with your life!

Dwimor This is really most unfair, your majesty.

Fruma You're a wizard, aren't you? Use some hocus-pocus and find him.

Dwimor If I may say so, your majesty, that is typical of the attitude of the general public towards the necromantic arts.

Fruma How dare you refer to me as the general public!

Dwimor Magic is a deep and difficult branch of learning. It is not just a matter of hocus-pocus.

Fruma Off with his head! That's it! I've had enough of his incompetence. Off with his head! Guards! Take him away!

Dwimor But, your majesty ——

Fruma No. No. No. No. No. Don't explain. You failed. You die. Guards!
Dwimor It's not my fault. Take your hands off me or I'll turn you into toads.
Fruma Take him away.
Dwimor No. No. Spare me! A few hours with my books and I'll tell you exactly where he is. It's the ingredients. You can't get the ingredients for the spells these days. I mean when did you last see a bat's wing in the grocer's? Be honest. They're a protected species. What am I supposed to do?

Prince Erfa limps in

Erfa What's all the fuss?
Dwimor However, as you're so concerned, I have brought him back to the palace as you see. (*He releases himself from the Guards and takes back the crystal ball*) I only wish you had a little more faith in me, your majesty. The prince is quite safe in my charge. I know exactly what he is doing at all times and protect him from all danger.

Erfa limps to the throne

Erfa I was attacked by six mysterious warriors.
Fruma What!
Dwimor As I knew of course, your majesty. There was no real danger.
Erfa They tried to kill me.
Dwimor Ha ha ha ha ha ha.
Fruma What are you laughing at? My son is nearly killed and you laugh!
Dwimor Well, if we didn't laugh we'd have to cry I always say.
Fruma Dwimor! I don't think you appreciate the situation. Prince Erfa is my *only* child. The heir to my kingdom. I am four hundred and eighty-seven years old.
Dwimor Your majesty is eternally youthful.
Fruma If anything happens to my son, then when I die, who will succeed to the throne?
Dwimor Your loyal subjects pray daily for your continued health, your majesty.
Fruma Who will succeed to the throne?
Dwimor Your wicked brother Snithan.

The Guards spring to attention and look around threateningly

Fruma Exactly. These warriors who attacked you, Erfa. Were they sent by Snithan?

Erfa They didn't say.

Dwimor They were probably just marauding brigands, your majesty, not expecting a royal prince to be walking alone in the wastelands of Scard.

Fruma Why *do* you disobey my instructions and leave the safety of the palace grounds alone?

Erfa Oh, Father, sometimes I feel that this palace is a prison to me. My gold chains and rich jewels are like shackles binding me. Despite all our power and riches I sometimes envy the ordinary subjects of the kingdom. Yes, Father, I have rank, I have honour, but there are times when I would change if I could. Times when I dream of no longer being a prince and a hero. No longer looked up to and admired for my strength, my nobility, my virtue and my beauty, but instead, this is my dream, to be — ordinary.

Fruma Ordinary!

Erfa Yes, Father, ordinary — because an ordinary man, Father, has something worth far more than gold. He has freedom. True freedom — something I fear that I shall never know. (*He hangs his head in a tragic pose*)

Fruma Freedom! You can have freedom. You can go anywhere you want. You can do anything you want. You have *carte blanche*.

Fruma takes two Guards by their arms and stations one on each side of Erfa

These two *ordinary* people, however, will lose their heads if they let you out of their sight.

The Guards look very alarmed and close in on Erfa even further

And now I have affairs of state to attend to.

Pause

I wish to leave.

The others look at each other, puzzled

Dwimor Is something detaining your majesty?

Fruma The fanfare. I'm the king. I can't leave without the fanfare.

Everyone bustles about. Fanfare, followed by ceremonial music

Fruma and most of the Guards process out

Two Guards remain with Erfa. Dwimor is looking into his crystal ball

Dwimor Your highness, I did not wish to alarm the king your father, but those warriors who attacked you were indeed soldiers of your wicked Uncle Snithan.

Erfa walks to one side. The Guards and Dwimor follow

Erfa My own uncle wants to kill me? Tell me, Dwimor. You have lived long. Tell me about Snithan. Many times I have asked my father. He will not speak of it. Why does my uncle live in exile in the mountains of Snutz?

Erfa walks. They follow

Dwimor In the twenty-fourth century, when your father and his brother were young men, each of them fell in love, as young men will.

Erfa blushes. He walks. The Guards follow

As fate would have it, they both fell in love with the same beautiful and enchanting maiden. Both wooed but she had eyes only for your father. The marriage was arranged and there was joy throughout the kingdom. But there was no joy in your uncle's heart. Jealousy and bitterness were effecting a change in your noble uncle's demeanour. It was as if his disappointment in love drove all the goodness out of his heart and left there only evil and a thirst for revenge.

Erfa walks. The Guards don't follow. They are hanging on Dwimor's every word. He motions to them. They follow Erfa

The day of the royal wedding drew near. All was prepared. Then, two days before the ceremony was to take place, the bride — vanished.
Erfa What do you mean?
Dwimor She disappeared. Could not be found. When her maid came to wake her the bed was empty.
Erfa Had she been murdered? Had my uncle ...?
Dwimor He was, of course, suspected. Your father had no doubt that his brother had kidnapped or murdered the bride. Snithan would say nothing. Had he not been a royal prince he would have been tortured to make him speak but as it was ... Your father exiled him to the ancient palace in the mountains of Snutz. He may never return on pain of death.

What became of the bride has never been discovered. Many years later your father married your mother, our dear late queen.

Erfa And Uncle Snithan?

Dwimor There are always rumours that he plots his revenge. Spies have been caught in the kingdom but little is heard of him.

Erfa Why do I not lead an army into the mountains of Snutz and put an end to his evil schemes?

Dwimor Your father would never allow it. Your life is too valuable to put at risk.

Erfa My safety! Always my safety! I cannot bear these restrictions.

Erfa attacks the Guards who flinch, but stay close

Dwimor But the attack today, your highness. Your uncle plans to kill you and if he failed today he will try again soon.

Erfa I am not afraid.

Dwimor Very commendable, your highness, but if you are killed, I will be executed and I do not share your royal courage.

Erfa I don't care, Dwimor. I will accept no further restrictions.

Dwimor But, your highness, I offer you freedom.

Erfa Freedom?

Dwimor The chance to be ... ordinary — as you wished.

Erfa Explain. I don't understand.

Dwimor One moment.

Dwimor takes the crystal ball and hands it to the Guards. He points at it. They look. We hear the title music from the children's TV show "Rainbow". They are riveted. Dwimor and Erfa step away from them

Your uncle seems determined to murder you. He is cunning. We may be unable to prevent him. The best way would be to catch him in the act.

Erfa Of murdering me?

Dwimor Exactly.

Erfa I thought you would not risk my life.

Dwimor I will not. I will risk the life of Brynmor.

Erfa Brynmor? Who is Brynmor?

Dwimor He is from another world. Let me explain. As you know, my receivers (*he points to the crystal ball*) intercept transmissions from other worlds, other dimensions. It was in this way that I discovered Brynmor. Look at this holographic image. (*He shows Erfa a piece of plastic*) Brynmor!

Erfa He looks exactly like me.

Dwimor Now you will see my plan. I use my necromantic skills to exchange you with him until your uncle's plans come to fruition and we can defeat him. You will have a taste of freedom. Brynmor is not a prince in his world. He is what you wished to be — an ordinary person.

Erfa Has he agreed to this?

Dwimor I was thinking of making it a surprise.

Erfa You're probably right. But will I not seem very out of place in this other world?

Dwimor That is a problem. Time is short — not long enough for detailed study. Take this volume and learn what you can about the people of Earth. The data banks show that it is by the man deemed to be their greatest writer. (*He gives Erfa a book*)

Erfa *William Shakespeare. The Complete Works.* Dwimor, I will start at once.

Erfa runs out. He comes back and whistles at the Guards. They follow him out. Dwimor takes the crystal ball and leaves to the title music of "Last of the Summer Wine"

Scene 4

Darkness

Hash Glastonbury is on a step-ladder changing the light bulb. Shaun is sitting at the table where the game is in progress

Hash OK, Donovan, you can turn it on now.

The Lights come up

Don enters

That's the last one. The whole house is now fitted with these new low energy light bulbs. Just as bright but they use less power. That should ease the demands on the generator. I hope the interruption didn't spoil your game.

Shaun No, Mr Glastonbury, we can't carry on until Bryn arrives.

Hash Mr Glastonbury! Shaun, we're all on first name terms in this house.

Shaun I don't know your first name, sir.

Hash Sir! The name is Hash. You can call me Hash.

Shaun That's an unusual name.

Hash More of a nickname really.

Don His real name's Nelson.

Hash I never liked it even as a child. Military associations. Bad vibrations. And then when it came to the sixties — Grosvenor Square, Aldermaston — well, I think your name is so much a part of your essential spirit, don't you?

Shaun Oh, yes.

Hash So some of my friends started calling me Hash.

Don (*meaningfully*) For some reason.

Hash For some reason, yes. And the name has stuck. It seemed to suit my — lifestyle. You can hardly imagine someone called Nelson being a Friend of the Earth, can you?

Daisy enters with a plate of cakes, drinks, etc., singing "White Rabbit" by Jefferson Airplane

Daisy Here you are. I baked some more of those fairy cakes.

Don Well don't let Shaun eat any. He started having hallucinations last time.

Hash Is this the nettle wine?

Daisy No, it's — daffodil.

Shaun and Don gag on theirs

Hash Daffodil? It must be years since we had this, Daisy. You know, Daisy, daffodil always reminds me of the first time we met.

Daisy Stonehenge.

Hash Summer solstice nineteen sixty-nine.

Hash and Daisy sing a line from "Aquarius" from the musical Hair. *They continue singing selections from the Flower Power songbook during the following*

Don Oh no. I hate it when they get like this.

Shaun And we haven't even started on the fairy cakes yet. (*He picks one up*)

Don Put that down.

Shaun Oh, Don.

Don (*gesturing towards the game*) You came here for an adventure.

Shaun These cakes *are* an adventure.

Don Sometimes, Shaun, I think you're a closet hippie. You'd *like* a permissive society, wouldn't you?

Shaun Well, they look happy. My parents are miserable, worrying about their share portfolios.

Hash and Daisy are now on "Good Morning Starshine" from the musical Hair

Don Isn't this a song from *Hair*?

Shaun I don't know. Why?

Don That usually means they start taking their clothes off.

Shaun Wow! You mean right here in front of us?

Don Anywhere. I swear I will *never* forget my tenth birthday party.

Doorbell

That'll be Bryn. Go and let him in, Shaun, while I deal with this situation.

Shaun goes out, sneaking a fairy cake as he does so

Mum, Dad. Will you please stop this?

Hash What's the matter, Donovan? We're enjoying ourselves.

Don Other people's parents don't still live in the nineteen sixties. What's the matter with you?

Daisy Donovan, your father and I believed in peace and love in the nineteen sixties and we still believe in them in the nineteen nineties. You don't change your beliefs according to fashion, like clothes. (*She looks at Hash's clothes*)

Don But you haven't changed your clothes either! Don't you realize it's embarrassing when my friends come round here and you're dressed up in caftans and flares and bells? How do you think I feel when they come round and see you like this? Don't you realize you look ridiculous?

Shaun and Bryn enter

Bryn is on his skateboard and executes one or two clever moves. He wears a Blue Peter *version of Erfa's costume. The gold belt and necklace are replaced by milk bottle tops strung together. The arm pieces are now badly painted washing-up liquid bottles. Instead of Erfa's boots Bryn wears a pair of wellies. Everyone stares at him*

Hash Er ... I think I hear the goat calling me. I'd better go and attend to it.

Hash goes

Daisy Yes, we'll leave you to your games, boys. Donovan, I didn't realize you had such interesting friends. (*She hands Bryn a fairy cake*) Have fun.

Daisy goes out singing "I Can Hear the Grass Grow" by the Move

Don stands staring at Bryn. Bryn smiles back and eats the cake

Bryn Are we ready, then? Do you like the costume? I copied it from one of those books you lent me. I had to improvise a bit. I thought it would help us to get into the spirit of it if we wore the appropriate costume. Why are you staring at me like that? Is it the swimming trunks? I haven't got any red ones. Apart from that, though, what do you think?
Shaun It's very nice, isn't it, Don?

Don stares, walks over to the drinks and pours himself a daffodil wine

Why don't we get on with the game. Come on, Don.

They all sit at the table

Don Are those milk bottle tops?
Bryn Yeah.
Don And these?
Bryn Washing-up liquid.
Don And wellies.
Bryn That was an inspiration.
Don Did your parents see you going out like that?
Bryn They're away for the weekend. Second honeymoon they call it.
Shaun Where have they gone? Somewhere romantic?
Bryn Yes. Abergele. So I'm on my own till Tuesday.
Don I thought you weren't very keen on the idea of these role-playing games?
Bryn That was before I came here yesterday. Now I realize that this is what I've wanted all my life.
Don To dress up in milk bottle tops and wellies?

Bryn No. To be a hero. I know I'm good at skateboarding and football and swimming — and cross-country running — and basketball — and gymnastics— but that's not enough, is it?

Don Er ... no.

Bryn Being a sports hero is not like being a real hero and fighting evil and defeating injustice, is it?

Shaun ⎱
Don ⎰   (*together*) Er ... no.

Bryn But with these games you can kind of act out your fantasies, can't you?

Shaun ⎱
Don ⎰   (*together*) Er ... yes.

Bryn So let's get on with it. I was just about to enter into combat with a malignant troll.

Shaun and Don turn their attention to the table. Black-out

Bryn leaves in the darkness to make a quick costume change. When ready he appears as Erfa

Shaun I think your father's everlasting low energy light bulb has gone.

Don Either that or the generator's packed in again.

Shaun No. It can't be the generator. I can still hear your mother's Grateful Dead record on the stereo.

Don I think my father left the other bulb over here somewhere. I'll see if I can find it and put it in. Will you turn it off at the switch, Shaun?

Shaun If I can find the switch.

There are noises of scraping chairs, stumbling, collisions, curses

I don't know how you cope with this happening all the time.

Don Have you got the switch?

Shaun I think so.

Click. Then very loud buzzing, clattering, siren noises

Don Turn it off. Turn it off!

Shaun What was that?

Don Well, it wasn't the light switch. It was my Star Trek Klingon destructor ray gun.

Shaun This must be the light switch.

Don Are you sure?

There is another strange noise. This is Dwimor's spell operating but they do not realize this. How could they?

Shaun What was that? Your Doctor Who Dalek disintegration beam?
Don I don't know. I haven't got anything that sounds like that. For goodness' sake hurry up and find the light switch.
Shaun That's it, definitely. You know, there's something spooky about your bedroom, Don. I haven't forgotten the last time.
Don OK. Switch on.

The Lights come up. Erfa is sitting exactly as Bryn was

Don Good. You've gone very quiet Bryn. Afraid of the dark?
Erfa Good-morrow, my friends.
Shaun You're not going to *talk* heroically too, are you?
Erfa I bring thee greetings from my native land.
Don OK. OK. If it helps you get into role.
Shaun Now, where were we? Oh yes, this malignant troll. Hey, does he remind you of anyone?
Don (*looking at a book*) No. Who?
Shaun Creepy Westmorland, our new maths teacher.
Don Oh yeah. I see what you mean.
Shaun Do you know what he did yesterday? Matthew Tiler fired a pellet at the blackboard while Westmorland was writing on it and he turned round and blamed me. Put me on detention next Tuesday. I'm not going though.
Don If you don't, you'll get put on report.
Shaun It's not fair.
Erfa Come take up arms against this Westmorland
       'Gainst foul injustice let thy hand be set.
Shaun Hit him, you mean? I don't think that would be a good idea.
Erfa What, shall we let this tyrant hold such sway?
       Such men have power but by our consent.
       Why shouldst thou pay thus for another's sin?
       In noble combat prove thy innocence.
Don Forget it. Let's get on with the game.
Erfa (*standing*)
       Thou thinkst that being young thou still hast time
       Time when in years to come thou art a man
       But courage is a plant that groweth not
       Without it be exposed to healthful sun
       Close hid, young shoots will wither and so die.

Don He's gone. It's these damned fairy cakes.
Shaun I don't think so. Look. (*He points at Erfa's clothing*)
Don (*embarrassed*) What?
Shaun They were blue. Now they're red.
Erfa If thou expect'st when that thou art a man
  To call upon a courage never tried
  No trusty oak of valour wilt thou find
  Weak rootless sapling courage will be thine.
Shaun And look at the belt. It's gold. What happened to the milk bottle
  tops?
Don And where are the wellies?
Shaun Something spooky's happening again!
Erfa If this vile Westmorland hath shamèd thee
  Let not thy vengeance wait upon thy doubt
  And if my arm be strong, thy cause be right
  Come follow me to Westmorland this night.

Erfa produces a sword from behind the table, raises it high and strides out

Don Where did he get that from? We'd better follow him.
Shaun I'm never coming to your house again!

Shaun picks up Bryn's skateboard and they chase after Erfa

SCENE 5

Snithan's castle

Snithan looks like Laurence Olivier as Richard III. Warriors stand on guard around the edges of the stage. Snithan is feeding his pets, called Scruffs. They are puppets and look like brightly coloured mop-heads. They make cute little squeaking noises

Snithan Ah, my friends, my only friends. How strange that I should hate
  my fellow men and yet feel such tenderness for these poor dumb
  creatures. In all this world only they do not hate me for my ugliness. And
  yet in the distant days of my youth I was considered handsome — that
  was before I was disfigured. That was before — the zit. (*He points to the
  end of his nose*)

One of the Scruffs has perched on a Warrior's shoulder. The Warrior tries to knock it off without being seen by Snithan

Guards!

They approach and stand to attention

(*To Warrior 1*) Now I am going to ask you a question and I want you to give me your honest answer. Do you understand?
Warrior 1 Yes, my lord.
Snithan Look at my nose. What do you see?
Warrior 1 My lord?
Snithan Answer the question. There, on my nose. What do you see?
Warrior 1 (*hesitating*) A zit, my lord.
Snithan (*angry, but controlling himself*) Good. You are a straightforward fellow. Very commendable. Now, another question and I want no prevarications. Would you describe the — zit — as an attractive feature?
Warrior 1 Er — no, my lord.
Snithan (*through clenched teeth*) And how *would* you describe it?
Warrior 1 Hideously ugly.
Snithan (*tautly*) Would you like to re-phrase that?
Warrior 1 Er — it's horrible — grotesque ...

The other Warriors are shaking their heads madly at Warrior 1

... repulsive — er — vomit-inducing. (*He is pleased with this last*)
Snithan Very honest. No beating about the bush with you, I see. Honesty is a rare quality nowadays and should be rewarded. Let me see. Yes, I think I shall award you my highest honour. (*He picks up a medal*) Allow me to pin it to your chest myself.

He does so. As the Warrior is bare-chested it causes him considerable pain. He faints

Take him away.

The Warriors carry out Warrior 1

When my brother and his repulsive brat have been disposed of and I am the ruler of this land ...

The Scruffs are nuzzling him affectionately

... zits will be compulsory. Those who cannot grow them naturally will have to buy artificial ones and stick them on. No-one will *dare* not to like me when I am king. My brother is old and sick. The boy, though, the boy must be eliminated. These fools, my guards, have failed. They are strong but brainless. I have a new plan.

The Scruffs are excited

And this time I will accompany them. We will infiltrate the royal guard at my brother's palace and strike the blow when he least expects it.

An old Crone bursts into the room and throws herself at his feet

Aaaaagh! What? Guards! I am being assassinated.
Crone I crave a boon. I crave a boon.
Snithan Help! Where are my guards?
Crone A boon, a boon. I crave a boon.
Snithan You crave a boon? (*He goes to the table, finds a dictionary and looks up "crave" and "boon"*) You want me to grant you a request?
Crone Yes, my lord. I crave a boon.
Snithan Guards!

The Warriors enter

Oh hallo. Good of you to come. I could have been carved into a thousand pieces!
Warrior 2 We were hoovering the battlements.

Snithan hits him

Snithan (*pointing to the Crone*) Get rid of this.

The Warriors pick her up

Crone But my boon, my boon.

There is a fight and she defeats the Warriors single-handed

Snithan I tell you what. I'll grant her a boon, shall I? Save bother?

The Warriors slink out, nursing wounds

What is it you want?

Crone I am an old woman, my lord, and my days are short. I have a son.
Snithan I will suspend my disbelief. Continue.
Crone I want to see him settled before I go. I am an old woman, my lord,
and my days are short.
Snithan Hurry up, then. What am I supposed to do?
Crone He has no skills, my lord. He is lazy and a simpleton. He is only
fit to be one of your lordship's bodyguards.
Snithan I think I've got an image problem here.
Crone Grant my boon, my lord.

He mouths following with her

I am an old woman and my days are short.
Snithan Where is your son?
Crone He waits without, my lord.
Snithan Bring him in.
Crone (*surprisingly loud*) Thor!

There are sounds of a door opening and heavy footsteps approaching

Thor appears. He is very small and thin

*Thor stops. The footsteps continue. He glares round at the effects depart-
ment. The footsteps stop. The Scruffs fall about laughing*

Snithan Isn't he a little on the small side for a bodyguard?
Crone He is small, my lord, but vicious.

Thor kicks a Scruff out into the audience

Snithan I'm not sure. I have to keep up some standards, you know.
Crone Oh, my lord, I am an old woman and ——
Snithan All right. All right. I'll give him an apprenticeship. I'll draw up
some indentures.
Crone (*hand to mouth*) You can borrow mine, my lord.
Snithan Don't be revolting! Thor, throw your mother out.

Thor does so with great enthusiasm

The Crone leaves

Now get down to the toyshop and get yourself a uniform. Guards!

Thor goes. The Warriors enter and line up

It is time to put my plan into execution. We leave for the royal palace in half an hour. Bring the scruffs.

Snithan marches out. The Warriors round up the Scruffs with considerable difficulty and slapstick chaos and leave

SCENE 6

The royal palace

Bryn wanders in, in a confused state

Bryn Shaun! Don! I don't think I'm in Greasby (*or local*) anymore! Why are there three moons? (*He shakes his head*) If I didn't know better, I'd say I was on another planet. It's Don's mother and her fairy cakes. I don't know what she puts into them.

Some Scruffs appear

Aaaaagh! (*He jumps up on to a throne*) Er — greetings — my name is Bryn ... I come from the planet Earth — er— I come in peace ...

Dwimor enters behind him

(*Without seeing him*) Er — we don't normally dress like this.
Dwimor Excuse me, Bryn.

Bryn jumps and turns

Bryn Aaaaagh! How do you know my name? Where am I?
Dwimor You are in Wuldor in the 327th year of the reign of King Fruma. I am Dwimor, the old wizard. I have brought you here because the kingdom has need of a hero.
Bryn (*pleased*) A hero?
Dwimor There is a threat against the life of our royal prince to whom you bear a remarkable resemblance not only in appearance but in strength, in nobility, in virtue.
Bryn Oh, thank you.

Dwimor I used my power to send him to the safety of your planet and brought you here so that his absence will not be noticed. Only you could take his place.

Bryn Only me?

Dwimor You will take the place of the prince until the threat to his life has been dealt with.

Bryn What exactly is the threat to his life?

Dwimor It is, of course, now a threat to *your* life. You will be the bait in my trap. Your wicked Uncle Snithan seeks to take over the kingdom on the death of his brother, your father. You are the only obstacle in his path.

Bryn How exactly does my uncle plan to kill me?

Dwimor I know not.

Bryn You know not! If you know not, how are you going to stop him killing me?

Dwimor It may be that I shall fail.

Bryn Oh yes?

Dwimor Better that you should die than that our beloved prince should fall.

Bryn Oh yes. Of course. Naturally.

Dwimor But you must be convincing. *Everyone* must believe that you are Prince Erfa. There is much that you must learn. To begin with ——

Fanfare

King Fruma enters

—— but there is not time. Here is the king, your father. He must believe you are Prince Erfa.

Fruma Where are the guards who were entrusted with your protection?

Dwimor Forgive them, your majesty. I have undertaken to protect the prince until supper.

Fruma And what will you do, Dwimor, should there be an attack? Wave your magic wand? Sprinkle some fairy dust? Erfa, what has happened to you?

Bryn Happened? I — er — well — er, nothing, Father. What do you mean?

Fruma Your clothing. You look ridiculous.

Bryn Oh, yes — well ...

Dwimor As always, your majesty, the prince is a leader rather than a follower of fashion.

Fruma What are those on your feet?

Bryn Wellies.

Dwimor A very practical new design of footwear that the prince hopes
will become popular.

Fruma Well, call me an old fuddy duddy (if you dare) but they do not quite
seem to lend the dignity one might expect in a member of the royal house.

A Guard enters

Guard Your majesty, the petitioners await an audience.

Fruma Is it time already? Let them enter in five minutes. I must first
assemble my regalia.

The Guard goes one way, Fruma the other

Bryn Did I fool him?

Dwimor It doesn't take much to fool the king but the real test will come
with Grongo.

Bryn Who's Grongo?

Dwimor Not who. What. Grongo is — er — a creature. In your world boys
have creatures called dogs as — er ...

Bryn Pets?

Dwimor Yes. Grongo is your pet, your inseparable companion. It is
Grongo I fear. He will know you are not his master but you must be seen
with him or there will be suspicions. The prince spent much time with
him.

Bryn Where is he now?

Dwimor He will be close by. I'm surprised we have not seen him yet.

There is a strange noise

Grongo enters. He is a large worm-like creature

Bryn shrinks back in horror

Bryn Grongo?

Dwimor Yes. Make friends with him.

Bryn approaches Grongo gingerly. He pats him

Bryn Nice boy.

*With a shriek Grongo attacks him. There is a huge struggle. Arms, legs and
wellies fly everywhere*

Fruma enters with his crown and sceptre and looks on, puzzled

Dwimor Ha ha ha ha. The prince so enjoys a romp.

Bryn is screaming, Grongo making bizarre noises

Fruma Erfa! The petitioners are approaching. Dignity. Before the peasants we must show dignity.

Bryn manages to extricate himself and Dwimor helps him to control Grongo who growls angrily

The Petitioners shuffle in

Let the first suppliant approach.

Peasant 1 Your majesty, I seek justice.

Fruma And justice you shall have. Who has wronged you?

Peasant 1 The Duke of Shadu. He is my landlord, your majesty. He wishes to knock down my house to extend his stables. He has raised my rent three times this year. He knows I cannot pay. Then he will evict me.

Fruma Say no more. I will speak to the duke. Your rent will remain at its former level.

Peasant 1 Your majesty is most gracious.

Peasant 2 comes forward

Peasant 2 Your majesty, I have been wronged.

Bryn He looks different.

Dwimor He is a Thrill.

Bryn Really? In what way exactly.

Dwimor He is of the race of Thrills. Inferior creatures.

Fruma Speak up. How do you think you have been wronged?

Peasant 2 I, too, am a tenant of the duke, my lord.

Fruma I suppose you've come snivelling about the rent, have you?

Bryn The king doesn't seem to like him.

Dwimor Nobody likes the Thrills. They are a worthless race. Always complaining.

Peasant 2 Your majesty, the duke has forbidden me to keep animals on my premises.

Fruma Well? That seems quite reasonable to me.

Peasant 2 But, your majesty, I run a stables. It is my livelihood. The duke is expanding his own stables. He wants to drive me out of business.

Fruma Oh, stop whinging. You people. You're just afraid of a little healthy competition. Get out.

Peasant 2 goes

Bryn But that's not fair.
Dwimor That's the great thing about being a king, isn't it? You don't have to be fair.
Bryn Where I come from we have a democracy. Everyone is equal. This couldn't happen there.
Dwimor Sounds very primitive.

Grongo attacks. The Lights fade as Dwimor and Bryn struggle with him

SCENE 7

Outside school

Jon is spraying NF on a wall

Don and Shaun appear and he runs off

Shaun Where is he?
Don I've left him in the toilets.
Shaun I'm still not sure I believe all that stuff about him and Bryn having swapped planets. Do you?
Don Well how else do you explain the gold and that sword? Where is the sword?
Shaun I hid it in their toolshed when I took him home last night. It's a good job Bryn's parents are away. The woman next door gave us a very funny look when we asked for the spare key.
Don What are we going to do with him? He insists on staying at school. And have you seen him on that skateboard? They're not even allowed in school.
Shaun A French exchange is one thing but this is ridiculous.
Don He wants to challenge Creepy Westmorland to combat.
Shaun Shall we let him?
Don No! When Bryn comes back — I suppose they will swap back — he'll get the blame for what this one does now.

Erfa enters on Bryn's skateboard. He executes some very spectacular moves on it. He is clearly a natural

Erfa How comes it, fellows, that we tarry here?
Where is this Westmorland I come to kill?

Shaun Kill?

Don No. Don't kill him just yet. Save your strength for the contest this afternoon.

Shaun What contest?

Don (*to Shaun*) The athletics match. (*To Erfa*) A mighty contest of strength is to take place between the heroes of our school and the heroes of Smart College.

Erfa Our enemies?

Shaun No. No. Not enemies. It's just a *friendly* contest. Nobody gets killed.

Don There are tests of strength and speed and skill.

Shaun (*with emphasis*) It's very peaceful.

Don And Bryn was down for several events so you'll have to take his place.

Don, Shaun and Erfa leave as Jan and Jon enter. Jan is carrying a large folder and a bag

Jan He said it would be worth an "E" if I improved the overall presentation.

Jon The best grade I've had for my coursework so far is an "F plus".

Jan And I spent half an hour on this one.

Jon Half an hour! I make it a rule never to spend more than ten minutes on any one piece of work. We've got to have some social life, haven't we?

Jan Yeah, what do they expect? There's more to life than exams, isn't there?

Jon It's that creep, Roy, who spoils it for the rest of us, too.

Jan We know what he'll get, don't we?

Jon }
Jan } (*together*) An "A".

Jon He got a "B plus" once and they had to talk him down off the roof of the science block. Said he couldn't live with the shame.

Jan I'd like to get hold of his coursework and — and — tear it into a thousand pieces.

Jon That's not a bad idea. It's only compared to his that ours looks bad. Without that we might get an "A".

Jan It's only a matter of opinion anyway.

Jon I think my work's worth at least a "B minus".

Jan I think yours is as good as mine and mine's worth an "A". Roy's just
a creepy swot.

Jon His work shouldn't be marked on the same scale. There should be a
special creepy swots' scale for him and all the other creepy swots.

Jan I bet if there was a creepy swots' scale he wouldn't do so well at all.
I bet he'd get a "C" or a "D".

Jon Yeah. And then they could have another scale for people like you and
me — the normal people.

Jon Yeah. On a normal people's scale I bet we'd do really well.

Jan It's not fair we have to compete against the creepy swots.

Jon So let's do it.

Jan What?

Jon Get Roy's coursework and rip it into a thousand pieces.

Jan Good idea. Keep an eye on him and see if he leaves it anywhere where
we can get at it.

Jon Right. Shh! Here come Bryn. What's he look like?

Erfa enters on a skateboard

Jan Lost your trousers?

Erfa Good-morrow, friends, pray tell me how to find
The house of Westmorland if it be near.

Jon You what?

Erfa Thou understandst me not, though I speak plain?
I seek one Westmorland. Knowest thou him?

Jan How long have you been wearing jewellery then?

Jon It suits him, though, doesn't it, Jan?

Jan I tell you what. He could do with a little more eye shadow.

They laugh

Don and Shaun enter looking for Erfa

Don Here he is.

Shaun Oh no. He's with Jon and Jan. And they're skitting him.

Erfa Mak'st thou mock of me, thou base-born slave?
Had I my weapon here 'twould cost thee dear.
I'd unseam thee from the nave to the chops.

Don Calm down, Bryn. They're only joking.

Jon If he wants a fight.

Shaun I wouldn't tangle with him if I ——

Jan Why's he running round in his underwear?

Shaun He's not been well.

Erfa Stand back! I'll brook no insult from this squab.
   Thou mockst my clothing and true I am in need
   A uniform like these I seek to wear
   And thou, for this abuse, shalt give me thine.
Jan What?
Erfa The uniform. Give it to me.
Jan You're joking, aren't you?
Shaun Bryn, now hang on.
Don No. Leave him. It'll solve the uniform problem.
Jan You're asking for trouble, Bryn.
Jon What's the matter with him?
Don Well, it's hard to explain.
Erfa The uniform!
Shaun Better give it to him. It's only for today. He'll get into trouble if
   he's seen like that.
Jan No chance.
Shaun Your class has got games after break and it's the match this
   afternoon. You don't *need* your uniform.
Erfa The uniform!
Jan Are you getting hard of hearing? You get the uniform over my dead
   body.
Shaun *Don't say that!*
Don Too late.

*Erfa attacks Jan. Jon tries to help Jan. Using brilliant skateboard
technique, Erfa manages to hold his own against them but eventually he
falls and the three become a heap of legs and fists*

   They roll off stage. Mr Westmorland enters

   Ah, Mr Westmorland.
Shaun (*aside*) Oh no. We've got to get rid of him quick.
Mr Westmorland Are those boys fighting?
Don No, sir. It's just a game. Er — American wrestling.
Shaun Look, sir. There's smoke coming from the windows of the senior
   toilets.
Mr Westmorland That'll be Mark Knoop and his cronies lighting up. I'll
   surprise them from the right flank. Thank you, Shaun.

   *Mr Westmorland goes. Erfa returns in school uniform, on the skate-
   board, and joins Don and Shaun. They adjust his tie and leave. Jon
   staggers on, concussed. Jan's head appears from the wings*

Jan Jon! Jon!

Jon staggers about, not hearing

Jon! Pass us me kit. In me bag there. Jon!

Jon staggers around

Jon! Please! I can't come out like this.

Jon staggers around

Jon! You dozy twollop! Bring me bag! Now!

Jon staggers out

Jan looks all around. He comes on, in his underwear, looking all around except at the audience. He gets the bag, tiptoes back, sees the audience and holds the bag in front to cover his embarrassment

Black-out

SCENE 8

The Plains of Guma

Snithan, Thor, Warriors and Scruffs are marching towards the royal palace. They stride on the spot. The Scruffs are singing a marching song

Snithan Halt!

He stops. The others fall over him

Thor Where are we, my lord?
Snithan These are the Plains of Guma.
Thor The Plains of Guma where no traveller is safe from the murderous attacks of the savage rebels of the Thrill tribes, those Plains of Guma?

The Warriors look around nervously

Snithan The Thrills are an inferior race, no match for warriors such as these. We will camp here for the night.

The Warriors unpack various items of domestic equipment, garden chairs, etc. They put a pot on the fire to cook. There is a strange howl. They all quake

Warriors The Thrills!

Snithan Pull yourselves together. They're just uldreegs calling to each other.

Thor Uldreegs — the giant flying creatures with razor sharp beaks and claws and ravenous appetites for fresh meat, those uldreegs?

Snithan They're terrified of fire. As long as we keep ours burning they will not come near.

Warrior 1 (*looking at the fire*) It's gone out!

Panic amongst the Warriors. They run around in all directions until the fire is relit

Snithan Now just calm down. Let's all just gather round the fire until the food is ready.

The Warriors and Scruffs form a circle round the fire. The Scruffs start to sing in their squeaky language. The Warriors clap along

Unnoticed, the Thrills emerge from the shadows and surround them

Eventually the Warriors notice. There is a fight which is inconclusive

The Thrills are driven off, chased by Snithan

A Scruff lies motionless. Thor approaches it. They all surround him. Thor listens for the Scruff's heartbeat, then holds a mirror up to its face. He shakes his head. All the Warriors stand, heads bowed

Snithan enters

He sees the Scruff, picks it up, throws it in the pot and gives it a vigorous stir. He takes up the song as before. The Warriors stare, horrified, as the Lights fade

CURTAIN

ACT II

Scene 1

The gym and changing-room at school

The Lights come up to reveal an impressive human pyramid of boys. They are, in fact, invisibly supported on blocks or scaffolding. Mr Westmorland supervises

Mr Westmorland No, I think it would be better if you were on the right hand side, Robinson, and you were on the left, Williams.

Two boys on the bottom row swap places while the pyramid remains miraculously intact

Yes, that's perfect. I should think everyone at the Open Day will be most impressed with that.

The Lights change

In the changing-room Jan and Jon are going through Roy's bag

Jon Hurry up. He'll notice we're missing in a minute.
Jan Here it is. One folder of grade "A" coursework. (*He takes out sheets of paper*)
Jon Do you think we should?

Long pause

Jan No, we shouldn't ... but we're going to anyway.
Jon Give me some.
Jan Not here, stupid. Then they'd know it was someone in our class. We'll just smuggle it out and he probably won't realize it's gone until later.
Jon Put it in my bag.
Jan No. If he does notice it's gone, Westmorland might search our bags. Better if we get someone else to take it out and we'll get it back from them.

Jon In someone else's bag, you mean?
Jan Yeah. Or in a coat pocket or something. (*He looks round*)

Erfa enters

Erfa A truant disposition, good my friends?
Jan Oh ... er ... look ... no hard feelings, eh?
Erfa I seek not entrance to a quarrel,
I bear news for thy schoolmaster from mine.
Where lies he?

Jan sneaks the coursework into Erfa's pocket

Jon Who? Westmorland? He's in there.
Erfa Westmorland?

Erfa strides off. Jan and Jon follow

The Lights change

The group are being gymnastic in the gym

Westmorland! I have found thee out!
Mr Westmorland Don't come barging in here shouting, lad. Where do
you think you are?
Erfa Thy time of life is short!
Down, down to Hell and say I sent thee thither.
Mr Westmorland And watch your language.

Erfa attacks Westmorland

He's gone mad! Bryn Masters! Don't tangle with me, lad. Now, I don't
want to hit you.

Erfa chases him round the gym

(*To the boys*) Well, don't just stand there. Get hold of him.

A struggle. Erfa is overpowered. The coursework falls out of his pocket

I've read about this. Teenage glue sniffers. I didn't expect to see it in this
school. What are all these papers?

Roy Sir, it's my coursework. It was in my bag in the changing-room. (*He collects it up*)

Mr Westmorland Well, that's something else you can explain to the headmaster. Keep hold of him, lads. We don't want him to do himself an injury.

The boys take Erfa out. Mr Westmorland follows. Shaun and Don arrive in time to see Erfa taken out. They follow

SCENE 2

The royal palace

The stage is full of Scruffs. One has a musical instrument. It plays. One starts to dance. Others join in. Eventually they are all dancing merrily. Towards the end of their performance Snithan enters and is horrified. He rushes around, restraining and shushing them

Snithan Are you trying to wake the whole palace? You can celebrate *after* I become ruler of the kingdom. Thor!

Thor enters

Have my men infiltrated the palace guard?

Thor Yes. It was easy. They were having a recruiting campaign.

Snithan It's the old wizard, I fear. He will not be so easy to fool. You must deal with him.

Thor Deal with the wizard? The wizard who can turn me into a toad with a wave of his wand — that wizard?

Snithan (*producing a bottle*) You must pour some of this liquid into his wine. It is a powerful drug which will put him to sleep while I deal with the royal brat.

Thor Wouldn't it be better to poison him? In case he might feel like taking revenge when he wakes up.

Snithan No. No. No. When I am king he will be very useful to me.

Dwimor, Bryn and Grongo enter

Here he comes with the brat. I must hide. He knows my face. Take this. I am relying on you. (*Aside, as he hides*) This could be a mistake.

Grongo is behaving aggressively towards Bryn

Bryn This creature is going to give the game away. Can't we lock it up somewhere?

Dwimor No. That would be even more suspicious. Everybody knows Grongo adores the prince.

Grongo bites Bryn

Perhaps the guards could look after him for a while. Guards!

Snithan's warriors enter, not looking very convincing as royal guards

Take charge of the royal pet.

A Guard attempts to put a collar and lead on Grongo. Others help him. It is a great struggle. Thor approaches Bryn and Dwimor with drugged wine

Thor Your majesty. Wise one.

He offers a tray with two drinks. They take them. Grongo lunges forward and knocks it out of his hand. It is obvious that it was deliberate. Bryn and Dwimor stare at him

Nervous reaction, your majesty. I will bring more wine.

Thor goes

Dwimor I don't remember seeing him before. In fact I don't remember seeing any of these guards before.

Thor returns with the wine

What's happened to all the old guards?

Thor Posted to other duties. The king has selected his crack troops from every regiment for the new royal bodyguard.

Bryn Crack troops?

Dwimor (*drinking, aside to Bryn*) I'm not happy about this. We must keep alert. (*He falls down, drugged*)

Bryn Dwimor!

Thor Grab him!

Guards overpower Bryn. Grongo assists them

Snithan enters

Snithan Excellent work.
Thor Shall we kill him now?
Snithan Why not? Right here in front of his precious pet. It will be a touching scene as the creature mourns over his master's body.

Grongo sinks his teeth into Bryn

Bryn Aaaagh! You vicious great slug! I'll ... (*He struggles*)
Thor Can I do the honours? (*He waves a knife threateningly*)
Snithan Wait. There's something wrong here. What's the matter with the animal? And why is he wearing these strange objects? This could be one of Dwimor's tricks. He is cunning. Tie him up. We'll take him back to the castle for interrogation.

They put a sack over him and tie him up

Thor and Snithan carry Bryn off

Only Dwimor and Grongo remain. Grongo tries to waken Dwimor and finally succeeds

Dwimor What's happened? Where's Bryn? (*He dashes over to his crystal ball and looks in it*)

The theme music from Blue Peter *plays*

(*Shaking the crystal ball*) Snithan! If he gets Bryn back to his castle, he'll get the whole story out of him. Quick. There's not a moment to lose.

Dwimor rushes out with Grongo

SCENE 3

The Glastonburys are putting finishing touches to the PA system

The Headmaster enters

Headmaster Ah! Mr and Mrs Glastonbury!
Daisy Daisy.
Hash Hash.

Headmaster It's very kind of you to help us out with the public address.
I always think it adds to the atmosphere — makes it more of an occasion.
Daisy Do you think we should have a little music until we get started?
Hash It's very easy to connect up the cassette player to the system.
Headmaster Why yes. That would be excellent.

The Headmaster goes

Hash puts on the tape. It is very loud sixties rock

The Headmaster dashes back

(*Shouting*) I think we're ready to start now. Would you announce the
first event please?

The music is turned off. Daisy announces with PA echo

Daisy All competitors for the third year hundred metres to the starting
line, please. Third year hundred metres.

The PA is switched off

Shaun, Don, and Erfa, who wears athletic kit, enter

Don So what did the Head say?
Erfa He spake most wrathfully.
Don   } (*together*) No. No. No.
Shaun
Shaun How many times do we have to tell you. We don't speak like
Shakespeare any more. He wrote four hundred years ago.
Erfa In just one lifetime your whole way of speaking has changed? You
are a remarkable people.
Don Just tell us what happened about the coursework.
Erfa He said he would postpone his decision until after this match.
Shaun He'll wait until you win all your races and then he'll expel you.
Don Only it will be Bryn who'll suffer for it when he gets back.
Daisy (*PA on*) And here are the results of the Open High Jump
competition. First place goes to Andrew Disley with a winning jump of
five point four metres.
Hash (*PA*) Man, that's *really* high.
Don Dad! Just announce the results.

Daisy (*PA*) First year. Two hundred metres. All competitors to the start, please. First year two hundred metres.

Hash (*PA*) Yeah. (*He sings a line from "Keep On Running" by The Spencer Davis Group*)

Don Mum! Not here, please.

Daisy Hash, dear, look. I think the headmaster wants to talk to us.

Hash Yeah. I think he was interested in my article on an alternative curriculum.

Daisy takes Hash away

Shaun What are we going to do about Roy's coursework then?

Don We've no idea who took it.

Erfa There were two boys in the changing-chamber. The pox-faced one with greasy hair and the tall one with the swart complexion.

Shaun That's a good description. All we need is a translation.

Erfa They are approaching yonder.

Jon and Jan enter

Don Jan and Jon! That's it. They're bound to be responsible.

Jon Responsible for what, *Donovan*? (*He gives a peace sign*)

Don Stealing Roy's coursework and planting it on Bryn.

Jan What if we did? What are you going to do about it?

Don Tell the head.

Don points to the PA system, indicating surreptitiously that Shaun should switch it on. Shaun doesn't understand

Jon That would only be your word against ours and he was caught red-handed with the evidence on him.

Don gestures. Shaun catches on. The following is amplified over the PA

Don But you planted the coursework on him. Bryn didn't know anything about it.

Jan You know that and we know that but you try proving it.

Don Why did you want Roy's coursework anyway? To copy it?

Jon No. To lose it.

Jan No-one would believe it was our work. It's grade "A".

Jon We're grade "E".

Jan I'm grade "F".
Don So you were going to destroy it?
Jon Yeah.
Jan But this is even better. Bryn gets expelled.
Jon And we can always get Roy's coursework another time.

The Headmaster enters with Daisy and Hash

Headmaster Parry! Ellwood! Not only are you envious, selfish, lazy, despicable cowards but you are also very, very stupid. You have just confessed your crime over the public address system and done heaven knows what damage to the reputation of the school! My office. At once.

Jon and Jan go

Daisy (*PA*) Competitors for the fourth year four hundred metres to the starting line, please. Fourth year four hundred metres.
Shaun Erfa — Bryn, that's you.
Don Over there. We need you to win this one. We're doing badly.
Headmaster Go out there and win for Calday. Go out there with a stout heart, a clear conscience and an unsullied name. I see them stand like greyhounds in the slips, straining upon the start. The game's afoot. Follow your spirit!
Erfa (*to Don*) I thought you said ——
Don Just go and run. I'll explain later.

Erfa goes

Hash gets to the microphone

Hash Everything's beautiful, man. I mean — all this grass. Beautiful, man.

He puts on psychedelic music: "Itchycoo Park" by The Small Faces. The Headmaster tries to switch it off. Don groans with embarrassment. Daisy dances a country dance

The Lights and sound fade slowly

SCENE 4

The plains of Guma

Snithan, Thor, Warriors, and Bryn (double) in a sack enter, travelling back to Snithan's castle. Thor is juggling, using three Scruffs. They stop for a rest

Thor Isn't this where we got attacked by the Thrills?
Snithan Yes, I think so. Don't worry. Lightning never strikes twice in the same place.
Thor Well that does it. You shouldn't have said that. You know what will happen now, don't you?
Snithan Sorry.

The Thrills attack again

Snithan and Thor beat them off, rendering their weapons useless by impaling Scruffs on the points. The Thrills lie nursing their wounds

Snithan, Thor, Warriors and Bryn leave. Dwimor and Grongo cross the stage, stalking Snithan

Dwimor Excuse me. You didn't happen to see a group of warriors led by a man with a hideously ugly zit on the end of his nose?

The Thrills look puzzled. They point in the direction Snithan went

Thank you so much.

They follow. Grongo treads on the wounded

SCENE 5

Don's bedroom

Don, Shaun and Erfa are sitting on the bed

Don So what's the matter, Erfa? You won every event. Bryn will be an even bigger hero when he gets back than before.

Erfa This is a matter on which we must speak.

Don What matter?

Erfa The return of your friend, Bryn.

Shaun Yes. How long will it be?

Erfa I should never have agreed to the exchange. *Every* life is of equal value. It is not right that your friend should die for me.

Shaun Die?

Don Bryn is dead?

Erfa Perhaps not yet but it is only a matter of time. Dwimor ——

Shaun (*to Don; explaining*) The old wizard.

Erfa — is using Bryn to bait a trap for my wicked Uncle Snithan who seeks to kill me so that he may rule the kingdom. There is a great danger and he deemed it best to risk Bryn's life rather than mine.

Don Did Bryn know this?

Erfa Not until it was too late.

Shaun Well, he said he wanted to be a real hero.

Don Can't you swap back somehow?

Erfa I have Dwimor's incantation to return myself at any time but I am to await his instructions. I cannot do anything about returning your friend to you.

Don Would this incantation work on us too?

Shaun Hold on.

Erfa I don't know. I expect so.

Shaun Let's just talk about this a minute.

Don What's to talk about? We have to go to Wuldor and rescue Bryn. (*He starts rummaging through a drawer*)

Shaun What are you looking for?

Don Swimming trunks.

Shaun The baths close at six on a Thursday.

Don Here we are. Which do you want, the yellow or the green? (*He holds up two pairs as he goes to the door*) Mum! Have you still got those milk bottle tops you were saving for the Greener Greasby Festival Fund?

Shaun We don't want to rush into anything.

Don Erfa, get changed.

Erfa starts to remove his school uniform to reveal his princely costume

Washing-up liquid bottles! Where will we get them at this time of night?

Daisy enters carrying a box of milk bottle tops

Daisy Here they are, dear. Are you making something for school?

Don Wellies!
Daisy I don't understand.
Don We need two pairs of wellies!
Daisy Well, your father has several pairs he uses for mucking out the goat
but they ——

Don dashes out

—— will probably be rather smelly. (*She looks quizzically at the other
two*)

*Erfa finishes removing his uniform and stands in an heroic pose. Daisy
looks at Shaun hoping for an explanation but he cannot find the words and
grins sheepishly and takes the box from her*

Don rushes in with two dirty pairs of wellies

Is it a play you're rehearsing?

Erfa produces his sword

I hope it's nothing too violent.

Hash enters

Hash Don, you can't go running off with my wellies. I need them.
Don There's no time to explain. It's an emergency. We have to get ready
quickly. Shaun and Erfa and I are going to another planet.
Hash (*enthusiastically*) Yeah!
Don No, not like that. We are literally going to another planet to rescue
Bryn.
Daisy But Bryn's here, dear.
Don No. This isn't Bryn. This is Erfa. They're doubles. They swapped
places. Bryn's life is in danger on Wuldor, that's the other planet, and
we have to go and help him. We need the milk bottle tops and the wellies
to wear so we won't look conspicuous.

Hash sings a line from "Mr Spaceman" by the Byrds

Daisy How are you getting to this other planet, dear? Is there a rocket or
something?

Don We'll use magic. Erfa has the incantation.

Erfa shows her a printed card. Hash sings a line from "Magic Carpet Ride" by Steppenwolf

Don Quick. Let's get changed.

Don drags out a reluctant Shaun

Daisy is making bottle tops into necklaces and belts

Hash You know there have been times when I've worried about that boy
— joining the cub scouts, doing well at all those competitive sports,
when he won that *Blue Peter* badge, but this is terrific. Going to another
world with a magic spell to rescue his friend from a race of evil warriors
— it's pure Tolkein. That boy's a real Glastonbury.
Daisy Hash, I've had an idea. Why don't we go too?
Hash Far out.
Erfa It might be dangerous.

Hash sings a line from "My Generation" by The Who

Daisy Oh, but dear, we haven't got any more wellies.
Hash (*to Erfa*) Will that matter?
Erfa Well, no. They're more for formal wear really.
Hash I'll wear my loon pants!

Hash dashes out, bumping into Don and Shaun who are entering

During the following, Don and Shaun are decorated with milk bottle tops

Don What about weapons?
Daisy Leave that to me.

Daisy dashes out

Erfa I think I'd better go first to check that it's all clear. You follow on
in five minutes. Here's the incantation. (*He hands Don the card*) I know
it by heart.
Don Good luck.
Shaun I knew something horrible would happen if I came in here again.

Erfa Are you sure you wish to take this risk?
Don We're sure. Just incant your incantation.
Erfa Very well. (*He stands on the skateboard and adopts a mystical pose and voice*) Durd da da doodle doodle dingle deet.

As he chants, his voice and the Lights both fade

SCENE 6

The kitchen at Snithan's castle

There is a large table and an oven. In the corner are sacks of vegetables

Snithan enters with Thor

Thor The kitchen! You're going to torture him in the kitchen! It's ridiculous. Why don't you get a proper torture chamber? There's a sale at MFI.
Snithan We know it's the kitchen but as far as the brat is concerned it's the torture chamber. It's dark and gloomy. There's fire and lots of sharp instruments. He'll never know the difference as long as we don't give the game away.

Bryn (substitute), still in the sack, is dragged in by Warriors

Put him in the corner next to the potatoes.
Thor The branding irons! Next to the branding irons.

The Prisoner is dumped in the corner next to the sacks

The Cook enters and starts to chop vegetables on the table paying no attention to the others

Snithan (*glaring at the Cook*) What are you doing?
Cook Preparing dinner.
Thor For the vultures! If the prisoner does not talk, they will dine well tonight.
Snithan What vultures? What are you talking about?
Thor (*with emphasis, pointing at the Prisoner*) The vultures that we feed the pieces of the dismembered prisoners to.
Cook Do you mind if I get on?
Thor No, chief torturer, make your gruesome preparations. Is your implement sharp enough?

Cook It's good enough for chopping carrots.

Thor Chopping carrots! Ha ha ha. Nicely put. You torturers do have a macabre sense of humour.

Cook What's funny about chopping carrots?

Thor Indeed it is no joke for those whose carrots are being chopped!

Cook Is there something I can do for you?

Thor Indeed there is. The prisoner may be stubborn. Prepare the rack, the thumb screws, the red hot needles and ... (*lost for ideas*) ... and ... the grinkling tool.

Cook Do you want Brussels sprouts?

Thor Have you *no* feelings, man?

Snithan Can we get on with this, please? Put the prisoner on the table.

Thor Rack!

Snithan Yes. The rack. Put the prisoner on the rack.

The Warriors pick up the sack and put it on the table. They open it and cabbages pour out

Cook How am I supposed to work in these conditions?

Snithan The other sack.

Warrior 1 (*inspecting the sacks*) These are all vegetables.

Snithan (*striding over*) I know he's not very bright but that's going a bit far. Where ...? He's gone.

Thor Quick. After him.

The Warriors rush out

Snithan He can't get far trussed up like that.

Thor (*indicating the mess on the table*) We need to get rid of all this. (*To the Cook*) We'll eat out tonight. (*He swipes everything off the table. He gives the Cook a torturer's mask and takes his chef's hat*) Put this on and look ruthless.

The Warriors bring in the real Bryn, still trussed up

Snithan Put him on the table.

Thor Rack!

They take off the sack and tie Bryn to the table

Snithan Now. There is something wrong here. I can't quite put my finger on it. Capturing you was just too easy. That old wizard, Dwimor, is up to something and I want to know what. So talk.

Bryn Never.
Snithan Chief torturer!

Pause. The Cook realizes this means him and looks bewildered

Cook Yes?
Snithan Loosen his tongue!

*The Cook looks at Thor who gestures that he should do something to Bryn.
The Cook looks round, lost for ideas. He produces a pepper pot and shakes
it in Bryn's face. Bryn sneezes*

Cook Talk.
Bryn Never.
Snithan (*sarcastically*) I think we might have to try something even more
   vicious, don't you?
Cook Tabasco sauce?
Snithan (*angrily*) How about something *sharp*!
Cook Lemon juice?
Snithan Try this. (*He hands the Cook an egg beater*)
Thor (*taking the egg beater and throwing it aside*) I think perhaps you'd
   better leave this to me. Leave me alone with him for half an hour and I'll
   get the information you want.
Snithan Very well.
Cook But do me a favour. I've got a strawberry soufflé in the oven which
   has to come out at exactly ——

Snithan hits him and pushes him out

Thor Now let's get down to business. To do a job properly I always say
   you need the right tools. (*He produces a cheese grater*)

*Bryn shrinks away with a gasp. This is repeated with a variety of kitchen
implements*

Bryn (*repeatedly*) No. I won't talk. Never. You'll never break me. What's
   that?
Thor This? Ha ha. This is my grinkling tool.
Bryn OK. OK. I'll talk. What do you want to know?
Thor Er ... everything.
Bryn OK. I was with Shaun and Don at Don's house and I was just about
   to encounter this malignant troll ——

Thor Wait there. I'll need to write this down. Pencil and paper.

Thor goes to get them

Bryn Fine hero I am. One look at a grinkling tool and I'm telling them everything. If I was a real hero I'd escape with a single bound. (*He strains and struggles against the ropes. No success*) Just a moment. I'll try using cunning. (*He removes his feet from his wellies which are tied to the table, and his wrists from the washing-up liquid containers*)

Bryn dashes out. He returns, removes the soufflé from the oven and dashes off

Black-out

Scene 7

The Plains of Guma

Dwimor and Grongo enter. Dwimor sits wearily

Dwimor I'm beginning to feel my age. Have to remember I'm not three hundred any more.

Grongo is agitated

OK. OK. I just need a minute.

Hash wanders in, carrying a rake and wearing even more outrageous sixties clothes than before. He looks round

Dwimor shrinks back. Grongo cowers behind him

Hash Hi. Have you seen a bunch of freaks with swords and stuff?

Dwimor stares apprehensively at him

Ha ha ha. This is far out. Do you understand me? Some kids and my old lady? Ha ha ha. (*He giggles throughout the following*) No. Let me explain. You're not getting this, are you? I can tell. Is this really another dimension? Woo! Set the controls for the heart of the sun, man. Ha ha ha. Hey, no, hey, listen. Take me to your leader. (*He is convulsed with laughter at this*)

Erfa (on a skateboard), Shaun, Don and Daisy enter armed with garden implements

Erfa Dwimor!

Grongo smothers Erfa with licks

Dwimor Your highness, you have returned. Who are these others? It is not safe for any of you here. Your uncle has captured the Earthboy and taken him to the castle.

Don Bryn's been captured? (*He brandishes a hoe angrily. To Daisy*) A hoe?

Daisy Best I could do at short notice.

Dwimor I fear that, under torture, he will tell all.

Shaun Torture!

Daisy Now look here. As members of Amnesty International we must ——

Hash Hey, this is great — Amnesty Intergalactical.

Erfa We must rescue Bryn.

Dwimor Your highness, you must not go. It is too dangerous. Leave it to me. I will make sure that he does not talk.

Erfa No, Dwimor. My life is no more important than anybody else's. I read that book you gave me — Shakespeare. "What a piece of work is man! How noble in reason! how infinite in faculty! in form, in moving, how express and admirable! in action how like an angel! in apprehension how like a god! the beauty of the world! the paragon of animals!"

Hash and Daisy sing a few lines of "We Shall Overcome"

Don (*interrupting them*) Mum. Dad.

Hash }
Daisy }   (*together*) Sorry.

Don No. Mum. Dad. You're right. All those crappy old songs you sing. They're right. We've got to stand up for what's right.

Shaun Let's go get Bryn.

Daisy And if this Snithan gives us any trouble ...

Hash (*giggling, brandishing the rake*) We'll rake him to pieces.

Everyone strides off, waving garden shears etc., Dwimor still protesting, Hash and Daisy singing "Suzanne" by Leonard Cohen

SCENE 8

The plains of Guma. Thrill camp

The Thrills sit eating round a campfire. Trum, their leader, leaps to his feet

Trum Thrills! Tonight you have feasted well.

Murmurs of agreement, licking of lips

Today our hunting has been successful. Tomorrow who knows?

Mithgrun (*an old bore*) "The Thrills are few and their days are as the leaves of the trees."

Trum Yes, indeed, Mithgrun, the wisdom of the ancients of our people. Our people who shared with the ancestors of Fruma the fruits of the earth and of the toil of men.

Mithgrun "The apple knows not the face of him who shall devour it."

Trum As we have often heard, Mithgrun, as we have often heard. How is it then that we, the once proud race of Thrills, we who walked as equals in the palaces and cities of this land, now live like this? Scarcely better than beasts.

Mithgrun "The vermin of wisdom are more worthy than the cattle of defeat."

Trum (*with an edge to his voice*) Indeed. We should never forget these simple truths. We are most grateful to you, Mithgrun, for your timely reminders.

Mithgrun "In the time of stillness come the words of comfort."

Trum (*gritted teeth*) Yes, but I was talking about the Sbills, the race of King Fruma. The Sbills who betrayed our ancient fathers and stole from us our birthright. The time has come for us to rise up and take back what is our own.

Mithgrun "That theft is good which reaches beyond cupidity."

Trum Shut up.

Mithgrun "The fool is deaf to the music of sincerity."

Trum hits him, knocking him out

Trum I am not a man of violence. We are not a people of violence. But we have submitted for too long to the tyranny of the Sbills. We must rise against them. We must fight for what belongs to us. We must defeat them wherever we can. We shall destroy them if we must but we shall have what is ours.

Cheers

Death to the Sbills!
All Death to the Sbills!
Trum Death to King Fruma!
All Death to King Fruma!
Trum Death to King Fruma!
All Death to King Fruma!
Trum Death to King Fruma!
All Death to King Fruma!
Trum Death to Prince Erfa!
All Death to Prince Erfa!

They are now in a frenzy

Bryn enters

Bryn Excuse me. I smelt food and I've been walking for hours. I wonder.
  Do you think I might ——
All Erfa!

*Bryn disappears under a heap of murderous enraged Thrills. He crawls
out from under them but they don't notice and batter on. He crawls to
where Mithgrun is just recovering consciousness*

Mithgrun *(to Bryn)* "Wise is the warrior who is mindful of the trees which
  grow by the river."
Bryn Are you a loony?

*The others notice Bryn and head towards him. Bryn seizes Mithgrun and
holds a knife to his throat*

Don't come any nearer or I will slit his throat.
Trum Is that a promise?
Thrill 1 No, Trum. Mithgrun is an elder of the tribe.
Bryn Now, just listen. I am not Prince Erfa. I am Bryn Masters and I come
  from another world, from Earth. It is a long story but you must let me
  explain.
Trum Very well. We will talk.

He and Bryn step aside and talk

Thrills 1 Well, Mithgrun, that was a close call.

Mithgrun "Danger is a plant with roots of ice."
Thrill 1 Oh, shut up.

Trum and Bryn step forward

Trum Now I understand.
Thrill 1 That was quick.
Trum We will help you. We will storm the castle of Snithan and remove the threat to your life.
Bryn Then I'll make sure the king will listen to your grievances.
Mithgrun "The rocks of the valleys show the mountains their way."
All Oh, shut up!

They leave in warlike activity

Scene 9

The kitchen at Snithan's castle

Snithan and Thor enter

Snithan Escaped! Escaped when you went for a pencil and paper?! (*He hits Thor*)
Thor Well, he was going to spill the beans.
Snithan (*with a look for spilt beans*) I don't care. He should have been incarcerated. (*He hits him*)
Thor That's a little extreme, isn't it?
Snithan Don't you realize, poltroon, that my whole plan depends on the destruction of Erfa?
Thor Well, why didn't we just kill him while we had him?
Snithan But *did* we have him?
Thor (*shouting*) Well, if we didn't why are you battering me for letting him escape! (*He realizes he has overstepped the mark*) Your grace. Sorry.
Snithan I'm sure that wizard has some scheme.
Thor Dwimor.
Snithan Yes. He is a cunning adversary, skilled and wily and able to surround himself with all the powerful spirits which his sorcery can command.

Dwimor, Erfa (on a skateboard), Shaun, Don, Hash and Daisy enter, armed with garden implements. Hash has a lawn-mower

Dwimor Snithan! Surrender or die!
Snithan Guards!

Warriors appear, without weapons

Warrior 1 Oh no. We're not re-landscaping the grounds again, are we?
Snithan Let me explain to you. These are our enemies. They have
   managed to get into the castle and they are planning to kill me. *Defend
   me!*
Warrior 1 If you wanted us to bring weapons, you should have *said...*

Hash steps forward with the lawn-mower

Hash (*laughing*) Surrender or we'll mow you down where you stand.
Snithan Never.

*Snithan picks up a ladle and hits Hash. A fight: garden implements versus
kitchen equipment*

   During it, Erfa changes places with a double

*Snithan and the Warriors win and put Erfa and the others in sacks and tie
them up*

Thor That was close. I very nearly got pruned.
Snithan This time we take no chances. Take this one (*meaning Erfa*) and
   — er — throw him in the mincer.

The Warriors start to take Erfa out

   They meet Bryn and Thrills in the doorway

Bryn Not so fast, Snithan.
Snithan But ... but ... you're ... he's ...
Thor A double!
Snithan Twins!
Warrior 1 There are two of them.
Thor Well, I think we've made that point fairly comprehensively.
Snithan Well, I don't care how many of you there are. We'll wipe you *all*
   out.

Another fight. Bryn and the Thrills are victorious, Snithan is killed

Bryn Let all traitors perish. (*He approaches Thor threateningly*)

Thor I was only obeying orders!

Bryn Don. Introduce him to your Black and Decker.

Don takes Thor out. There are screams, off

Dwimor (*to Trum*) You have saved the life of Prince Erfa and shall be well rewarded.

Trum There is only one reward for which we have fought — the emancipation of our people (*to Bryn*) as you have promised.

Bryn It's not me you have to deal with. It's time for us to return home. Where's Don?

Don returns, wiping blood from his Black and Decker

Dwimor All the people of Wuldor owe you their thanks.

Shaun Yes, but can we go home now, please?

Dwimor I will begin the incantation. "Durd dee da da doodle doodle dingle deet."

Hash and Daisy sing a line from "Do Wah Diddy Diddy" by Manfred Mann

Please! (*He incants on*)

The Lights fade

The Earth people exit

The Lights snap back on

A Messenger rushes in

Messenger I have grave news.

Dwimor Speak.

Messenger The king is dead.

Trum He was no friend to my people but he was a brave warrior and we will honour his memory.

Dwimor I think you will find the new king will end the subjugation of your race.

Trum Where is the prince? I mean the king.

Dwimor "Great thing of us forgot". They tied him in a sack. Over there.

Two Thrills bring forward the sack and start to untie it

Dwimor Your majesty, your father has passed away. You are now the
ruler of all Wuldor.

The sack is opened to reveal cabbages and potatoes

Your majesty? Don't tell me I got the incantation wrong again. I do have
a tendency to turn people back into vegetables I'm afraid.

Another sack jumps on. There is muffled shouting

The sack is opened and Erfa gets out

Erfa Dwimor, you are a stupid old fossil. What are you?
Dwimor A stupid old fossil, your majesty.
Erfa Trum, I owe my life to you and your people. I promise you that while
I rule the Thrills shall never again suffer degradation and ignominy. In
my administration we'll try to get as many Thrills as we can. In Wuldor
all shall be equal — except me, of course. When's the coronation, then?
After supper? I think the banqueting hall's that way.

All head for the exit indicated

Oy!

They stop

Let's just remember who's king here, shall we? After me, I think is the
usual arrangement.

*The Lights fade as Erfa takes the skateboard from the sack and leads the
way out on it*

SCENE 10

*The Lights come up on Shaun, lying on the bed wearing normal clothes.
He wakes*

Shaun Oh, thank heavens for that. It was only a dream. A nightmare. Wait
a minute. This is Don's bedroom. What was I doing in Don's bed? Don!
Where is he? Where is everybody? I hate all this, you know. Mysterious

things happening. Wizards and creatures and fighting. I like things to be normal. I like a routine. Eleven o'clock every Wednesday — double chemistry. Predictable. Safe. I get nervous when unexpected things keep happening. And it's always Don's bedroom. And here I am in it all alone. Don! Where are you?

Don, Bryn, Hash and Daisy enter

Don What's the matter?

Shaun I'm totally confused. Have we just come back from Wuldor?

Hash Let's get down to that kitchen and cook up some more of these cakes. They're out of sight.

Daisy I tried a little something new in the icing. I feel as if I've been on another planet.

Don We have been on another planet.

Daisy Yeah.

Hash Far out.

Bryn Have they been at it again with the — you know — the geraniums?

Don No. It wasn't the cakes. It was *real*.

Shaun That's what I was afraid of. It's this place. It all started with that man in a grey suit.

Bryn What man in a grey suit?

Shaun That's the whole point. None of you saw him! A man in a grey suit just appears in your bedroom and you don't even notice! And then we meet an alien being from another planet and we have to take him to school with us and then we have to dress up in swimming trunks and garden shears and travel through space and storm castles and fight warriors and there are wizards and little funny blobs that walk and a big worm creature and I think I'm going out of my mind. (*He breaks down in sobs*)

Don Shaun. Shaun. Calm down. You're not losing your mind. It was all real. All those things happened. We defeated Snithan and his warriors but it's all over now. We're back home safe and sound. We can just get back to our normal lives. Everyday routine. Double chemistry on Wednesdays. So just take it easy. Everything will be all right.

Shaun No more adventures?

Don No more adventures.

Shaun No wizards?

Don No wizards.

All except Shaun freeze at this point

The man from "The Moonlight Zone" enters behind Shaun

Shaun does not see him

Shaun No wormy creatures?

No response from frozen Don

Don? No wormy creatures? Don? What's the matter?
Man (*to the audience*) In the world of fantasy who is to say ——

Shaun shrieks, stares in horror at the frozen cast and at the man. He gets into bed and pulls the blankets over his head and sobs. During the following, the Lights fade to a spot on the Man

—— what is real and what is not? These ordinary people, called to another world to help those of whose existence they had never dreamed, will never doubt that there are worlds beyond this world, that there are lives beyond these lives, that it is not so far as they once believed from here —— to the Moonlight Zone.

Black-out

CURTAIN

FURNITURE AND PROPERTY LIST

ACT I
Scene 1

On stage: Nil

Off stage: Sword **(Prince Erfa)**
Weapons **(Warriors)**

Scene 2

On stage: Table. *On it*: board game, booklet, practical torches
Chairs
Fighting Fantasy posters on the walls

Off stage: Skateboard **(Bryn)**
Tray with cakes, etc. **(Daisy)**
Drinks **(Daisy)**

Scene 3

On stage: Two thrones

Off stage: Crystal ball **(Dwimor)**

Personal: **Fruma**: walking stick
Dwimor: piece of plastic

Scene 4

On stage: Table. *On it*: board game, booklet. *Behind it*: sword
Chairs
Fighting Fantasy posters on walls
Step-ladder
Light bulb (for **Hash**)

Off stage: Plate of cakes, drinks, etc. **(Daisy)**
Skateboard **(Bryn)**

SCENE 5

On stage: Scruffs
             Medals
             Dictionary

SCENE 6

On stage: Two thrones

Personal: **Fruma**: crown, sceptre

SCENE 7

On stage: Wall

Off stage: Aerosol tin of paint (**Jon**)
              Skateboard (**Erfa**)
              Bag, large folder (**Jan**)

SCENE 8

On stage: Scruffs
             Garden chairs, etc.
             Pots, etc.
             Camp fire

Personal: **Thor**: mirror

ACT II
SCENE 1

On stage: Blocks or scaffolding
             Roy's bag containing sheets of paper

SCENE 2

On stage: Scruffs
             Musical instrument for Scruff
             Tray with two glasses of wine
             Sack and string
             Crystal ball

Off stage: Collar and lead (**Guard**)
              Glasses of wine (**Thor**)

Personal: **Snithan**: small bottle
              Thor: knife

SCENE 3

On stage: PA system, including practical microphone, with cassette deck

SCENE 4

On stage: Nil

Off stage: Scruffs (**Snithan** and **Thor**)
              Weapons (**Thrills**)

SCENE 5

On stage: Chest of drawers containing two pairs of swimming trunks
              Bed
              Table. *On it*: board game, booklet
              Chairs
              Fighting Fantasy posters on walls
              Skateboard

Off stage: Box of milk bottle tops (**Daisy**)
              Two pairs of dirty Wellingtons (**Don**)

Personal: **Erfa**: sword, printed card

SCENE 6

On stage: Large table. *On it*: knife, vegetables, pepper pot, egg beater, cheese
              grater, ladle, etc.
              Oven. *In it*: soufflé
              Sacks of cabbages and potatoes
              Sacks, rope

Personal: **Thor**: torturer's mask

SCENE 7

On stage: Nil

Off stage: Rake (**Hash**)
              Garden implements, including hoe and shears (**Erfa, Shaun, Don, Daisy**)
              Skateboard (**Erfa**)

SCENE 8

On stage: Campfire

Personal: **Bryn**: knife

SCENE 9

On stage: As Scene 6

Off stage: Skateboard (**Erfa**)
              Garden implements including, hoe and shears (**Erfa, Shaun, Don, Daisy**)
              Lawn-mower (**Hash**)
              Black and Decker, bloodstained cloth (**Don**)

SCENE 10

On stage: Chest of drawers
              Bed. *On it*: blankets
              Table. *On it*: board game, booklet
              Chairs
              Fighting Fantasy posters on walls

LIGHTING PLOT

Practical fittings required: pendant light for **Don**'s bedroom

ACT I, SCENE 1

To open: Dim lighting

Cue 1	**Erfa** walks off, wounded *Fade to black-out*	(Page 1)

ACT I, SCENE 2

To open: Black-out

Cue 2	**Don**: "... electricity from the national grid." *Bring up lighting on Don's bedroom*	(Page 2)
Cue 3	**Shaun**: " ... is going to happen." *Black-out*	(Page 6)

ACT I, SCENE 3

To open : General lighting on royal palace

No cues

ACT I, SCENE 4

To open: Black-out

Cue 4	**Hash**: " ... you can turn it on now." *Bring up lighting on bedroom, practical on*	(Page 12)
Cue 5	**Shaun** and **Don** turn their attention to the table *Black-out*	(Page 16)
Cue 6	**Don**: "OK. Switch on." *Bring up lighting as cue 4*	(Page 17)

ACT I, Scene 5

To open: General lighting on **Snithan**'s castle

No cues

ACT I, Scene 6

To open: General lighting on royal palace

Cue 7	**Dwimor** and **Bryn** struggle with **Grongo** *Fade to black-out*	(Page 26)

ACT I, Scene 7

To open: General lighting

Cue 8	**Jan** holds the bag in front *Black-out*	(Page 30)

ACT I, Scene 8

To open: General lighting

Cue 9	**Warriors** light the fire *Fireglow; fade after short time*	(Page 31)
Cue 10	The fire is relit *Bring up fireglow*	(Page 31)
Cue 11	The **Warriors** stare, horrified *Fade to black-out*	(Page 31)

ACT II, Scene 1

To open: Lighting on gym area

Cue 12	**Mr Westmorland**: "... impressed with that." *Cross fade to changing-room area*	(Page 32)

Cue 13   **Erfa** strides off. **Jan** and **Jon** follow   (Page 33)
        Cross fade to the gym

ACT II, Scene 2

To open: General lighting on royal palace

No cues

ACT II, Scene 3

To open: General lighting

Cue 14   **Daisy** dances a country dance   (Page 39)
        Slow fade to black-out

ACT II, Scene 4

To open: General lighting

No cues

ACT II, Scene 5

To open: General lighting on **Don's** bedroom

Cue 15   **Erfa** chants   (Page 44)
        Fade to black-out

ACT II, Scene 6

To open: General lighting on kitchen area

Cue 16   **Bryn** dashes off   (Page 47)
        Black-out

ACT II, Scene 7

To open: General lighting

No cues

ACT II, Scene 8

To open: Dim lighting, fireglow effect

No cues

ACT II, Scene 9

To open: General lighting on kitchen area

Cue 17   **Dwlmor**: "Please!" (He incants on)   (Page 53)
            Fade to black-out; when ready, snap on previous lighting

Cue 18   **Erfa** leads the way out   (Page 54)
            Fade to black-out

ACT II, Scene 10

To open: General lighting **Don**'s bedroom

Cue 19   As the **Man** speaks   (Page 56)
            Fade to spot on **Man**

Cue 20   **Man**: "... to the Moonlight Zone."   (Page 56)
            Black-out

EFFECTS PLOT

ACT I

Cue 1	To open *Pulsating music; continue till end of Scene 1*	(Page 1)
Cue 2	**Man**: "... a journey to ..." *Dramatic chord*	(Page 5)
Cue 3	To open Scene 3 *Fanfare; ceremonial music*	(Page 6)
Cue 4	**Dwlmor** hands the crystal ball to **Fruma** *"Neighbours" theme tune*	(Page 7)
Cue 5	Everyone bustles about *Fanfare; ceremonial music*	(Page 9)
Cue 6	**Dwlmor** points at the crystal ball *Title music from "Rainbow"*	(Page 11)
Cue 7	**Dwlmor** exits *Title music from "Last of the Summer Wine"*	(Page 12)
Cue 8	**Don**: " ... my tenth birthday party." *Doorbell*	(Page 14)
Cue 9	**Shaun**: "I think so." *Click, very loud buzzing, clattering, siren noises*	(Page 16)
Cue 10	**Don**: "Are you sure?" *Strange noise*	(Page 16)
Cue 11	**Crone**: "Thor!" *Door opens, heavy footsteps approach; continue footsteps*	(Page 21)
Cue 12	**Thor** glares round *Footsteps stop*	(Page 21)

Printed in Great Britain by
Hobbs the Printers Ltd, Totton, Hampshire SO40 3WX

www.ingramcontent.com/pod-product-compliance
Lightning Source LLC
LaVergne TN
LVHW051800080426
835511LV00018B/3368